Things I Thought
When I Was 34

Lyle Kilbane

BookLeaf
Publishing

Things I Thought When I Was 34 © 2022
Lyle Kilbane

Presentation by *BookLeaf Publishing*

Web: www.bookleafpub.com

E-mail: info@bookleafpub.com

ISBN: 9789357696654

First edition 2022

For Joni and B.B.

Cathedral On The Hill

You shouldn't be able to touch the roof,
But if you can, make sure it's here.
Make sure it's Saturday at 3 o'clock,
Or make sure it's at night, under the lights,
Make sure your senses are overloaded,
Make sure the sound of music courses through you,
As eleven global Local Heroes touch grass,
Make sure the waft of Bovril or a grape vape lingers
in your nostrils.

Make sure the stresses of the week lift from your
shoulders,
And make sure no one needs to get in touch,
Make sure this is your life for ninety minutes,
Make sure you remember how you felt when the ball
hit the net,
Make sure you remember.

You shouldn't be able to touch the roof,
But if you can, make sure it's here.

January

A new year begins, full of wonder, full of uncertainty,
The worst is yet to come.

Recovery from COVID, back to normality,
The dreams of a life before the pandemic,
The worst is yet to come.

The post-Christmas blues,
The cold weather, the dark nights,
A glimmer of hope,
A light at the end of the tunnel,
But the worst was yet to come.

February

War.
An invasion in Europe,
A disaster in Ukraine,
The Russians are coming,
The Russians were here.

The clouds gather over Ukraine,
As the helpless world watched on,
Disaster and atrocity,
Brought to bear by a madman,
A gangster emboldened by the apathetic,
Or the enablers.

Slava Ukraini, Glory To Ukraine.

March

Beware.
Artificial snow in an artificial Games,
Nothing can replace the noise of war,
the pain of war, the cruelty of war.

The pain spreads like a virus,
All too familiar,
All so different.

Helpless and hopeless,
The brave fight,
The viewers watch,
The revolution may not be televised,
But misery always will.

April

Budget for the future,
Wish you'd saved in the past,
War costs a fortune,
But for the people, the money never lasts.

The price of existing ever-rising,
The cost of living,
Too poor to live.

The cost of war, the cost of profiteering,
Recoup your losses,
From those with no more left to lose.

May

Stefania.

The light in the darkness of an ever-darkening world,
A symbol of unity, a token of support,
Symbols can't be eaten,
And tokens won't slay an advancing enemy,
But a warm glow fills Europe for one night,
The glow of bombs, fires, destruction, despair,
Will return.

But Stefania will always have her night.

June

The problem with cracking up is you never know
when it's going to happen,
You never know when the darkness will descend,
When you won't want to get out of bed.

Surviving becomes a one-man war,
Living was hard when it was cheaper, it's more
expensive now.

Time is the answer,
The fog lifts, and normality returns,
Happiness, a smile that doesn't ache,
But time ticks so slowly,
When you're cracking up.

July - The Wedding

A lifetime in a day,
A whirlwind of emotions, tears flowing - willing
them to stop,
Let them flow, do as you please,
It's your day.

It's our day,
Our day to stand in the spotlight,
Our day to turn heads,
Our day to have and to hold.

The sunshine, the campervan, the harbour, the rings,
The sight of you walking towards me,
Never feeling happier,
Never feeling more alone,
Until you're with me and take my hand.

Then it's us and it's forever,
LOVE AND BE LOVED!

A Fine Day

It's a fine day for a caper,
A fine day for a fine piece,
An awffa fine day for a fly cup,
And a fine day for aw three.

It's a fine day for a wonder,
A fine day for a bosie
It's a fine day for a wander,
And a fine day for aw three.

It's aye a fine day where the mountains meet the sea,
A fine day for a fine life, fine folk, fine friends,
And a fine day for aw three.

August

Is it just me or is it getting darker earlier?
How soon in August can I get this question out?
15 minutes earlier every week from the summer
solstice,
That's what I've been told,
I never thought to check.

I could stand the world being completely fucked
when it was lighter,
This is just getting depressing.

September

The great leveller that comes for us all,
and so it came for The Queen.

An inevitable inevitability, proceeded by inevitable
pageantry,
A mother, a granny, an institution,
The people mourned while the people couldn't afford
life anymore,
How much does all this cost?

Nobody's judging,
That's the way it's always been.
A lot of effort for those deemed worth the effort,
For everyone else?
Just make an effort.

October

It came, it went,
31 days is too long for a month.

Have a word.

November

A winter World Cup,
A camel in the snow,
A Scottish accent on the network,
A gauntlet for a crow.

A space shuttle to Camber Sands,
An ice cube in your port,
Joelinton as a number nine,
A billionaire in court.

A regatta in a bathtub,
Cola in your tea,
A birthday cake for Halloween,
A padlock with no key.

A nightmare catcher in your room,
Some catnip for a pup,
A firework in the bright sunshine,
A winter World Cup.

December - In the future

These were written in November,
A dark, cold, uncertain November.
This is a look to the future,
A dark, cold, uncertain future.

December is the warmth, the hope that the best
is yet to come,
Christmas and Benidorm for me and you,
The best is yet to come,
The best will always come.

Or it won't...

I hope England didn't win the World Cup.

A Country Song

When you wake and face another hazy day,
Choices are flashing through your mind,
Be they big, be they small, be they nothing, be they all,
In time you're gonna know which ones to make

Take a right,
Take a ride
Take on anything you like,
Take the night,
Take the light,
Take your kids and your ex-wife,
Take a knee,
Make believe in what you want this world to be,
But you can't spread your wings in flight,
If you don't first take a right

How you gonna be a failure,
If you never learn to fail?
How you gonna ride the ocean,
Without a boat and setting sail?
You can't put off til tomorrow,
What you want to do today,
Life will pass on by you,
'Cause tomorrow's always a day away

Take a right,
Take a ride
Take on anything you like,
Take the night,
Take the light,
Take your kids and your ex-wife,
Take a knee,

Make believe in what you want this world to be,
But you can't spread your wings in flight,
If you don't first take a right

Saddle up your horses if you wanna head out west,
Find the love of your life, settle down and take a rest,
Write a country song and sell it,
If you think that would be best,

Take a right,
Take a ride,
Take on anything you like…

Two things in life are certain,
and the only one for sure is death,
So let's start living for the moment,
All it takes is one deep breath and...

Take the night,
Take the light,
Take your kids and your ex-wife,
Take a knee,
Make believe in what you want this world to be,
But you can't spread your wings in flight,
If you don't first take a right

Take a right,
Take a ride
Take on anything you like,
Take the night,
Take the light,
Take your kids and your ex-wife,
Take a knee,
Make believe in what you want this world to be,
But you can't spread your wings in flight,
If you don't first take a right

On Yer Erse

Yer on yer erse,
Not a pot to piss in,
Barely a piss to piss,
Nae money for the leccy,
Nae bidey in for a kiss

Yer on yer erse,
You've nothin',
Nothin' tae gie and naebody to gie it tae.

We could have had chaos,
Uncertainty, anxiety, needless worry,
Instead, we got the lot,
But coloured blue

Yer on yer erse,
And we aw are too

Eggs On Legs

Some eggs have legs,
Some eggs have none,
Some eggs love rain,
Some eggs love sun,
Some eggs are brown,
Some eggs are white,
No matter the colour,
All eggs are alright.

The Kingdom

Kilmany, Kilrenny, Valleyfield High and Low,
Blebo Craigs, Balmalcolm, Balmerino.

Crossgates, Cupar, Newport-on-Tay,
Gauldry, Gateside, the Isle of May.

Innerleven, Inverkeithing, Methil no more,
Ballingry, Lochgelly, The Meedies at Lochore.

Aberdour, Arncroach, Abercrombie,
The Links Market doon Kirkcaldy.

Starks, East End, Central old and New,
Or climb the tree and see the sea at mighty Bayview.

St Andrews, St Monans, Sir Jimmy Shand,
Rab Noakes, Barbara Dickson, Nazareth (the band).

Carnock, Cowdenbeath, Ceres, and Collessie,
Pittenweem, Carnbee, Elie and Earlsferry.

Radernie, Ravenscraig, Rosyth, Star,
Lumphinnans, Limekilns, Anster Fish Bar.

Ben in tae the scullery or up Norman's Law,
A barry time aw the time with yer neebers or yer
maw.

Kings were born in oor ain city,
Where The Abbeyview Buckfast Crew now rule,

David, Malcolm, Robert The Bruce,
Dairsie, Markinch, Auchertool.

The Witches' Cave, The Bunnet Stane,
Falkland, The Lomonds, hame.

What Snooker Ball Would You Eat?

If you had to, if someone put a gun to your head,
What colour snooker ball would you eat?

No, there's no talking your way out of it,
You have to eat the snooker ball.

Red is like a tomato, juicy, ripe, good for you,
Yellow, a lemon, bitter, I doubt you're choosing that
Green just screams health, a big sprout,
Brown, chocolate obviously, I hope you thought of
chocolate.

Blue, if you pick blue you need to have a long look at
your life,
Pink, a big mashed-up Starburst,
Black, liquorice - an acquired taste.

What about the cue ball?
A white egg? A whole bulb of garlic? That's almost
as bad as picking blue.

So think about it, ask your friends,
If they had to, absolutely had to,
What colour snooker ball would they eat?

2023?

Worse? Better?
The planet's dying so what does it matter?

Not much happens in odd-numbered years,
Unless it's 1939, 1945, 1963, 2001,
Or any of the others when things happened.

Take it a day at a time,
It is what it is,
Until it's not,
But until then, life goes on,
Let's hope for a quiet odd-numbered year.

Finale

There will be no encore.

Ingram Content Group UK Ltd.
Milton Keynes UK
UKHW020816060623
422954UK00016B/981

9 789357 696654